ATLANTA FALCONS

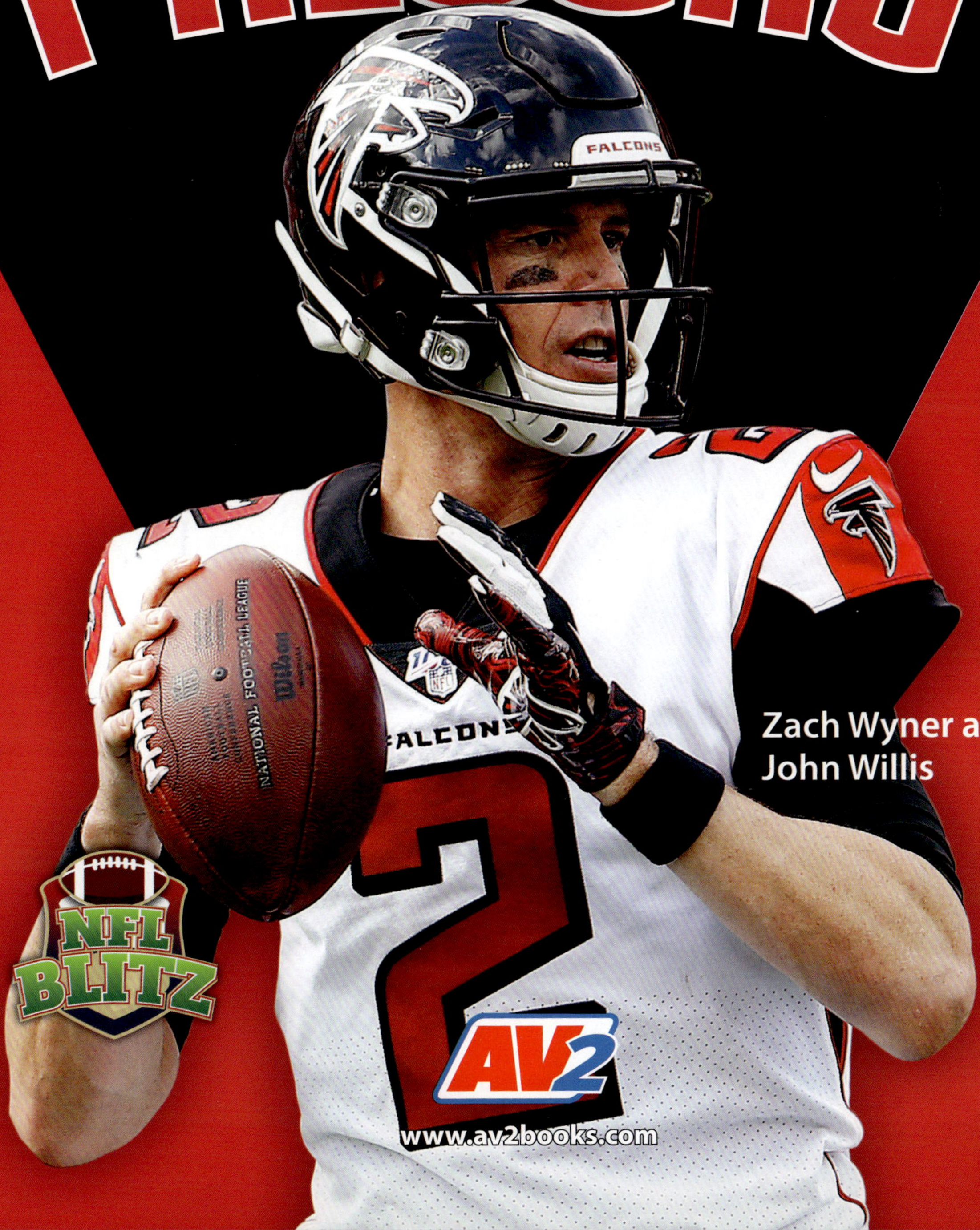

Zach Wyner and
John Willis

NFL BLITZ

AV2
www.av2books.com

AV2

Step 1
Go to **www.av2books.com**

Step 2
Enter this unique code
UWZANQHRP

Step 3
Explore your interactive eBook!

AV2 is optimized for use on any device

Your interactive eBook comes with...

Contents
Browse a live contents page to easily navigate through resources

Audio
Listen to sections of the book read aloud

Videos
Watch informative video clips

Weblinks
Gain additional information for research

Slideshows
View images and captions

Try This!
Complete activities and hands-on experiments

Key Words
Study vocabulary, and complete a matching word activity

Quizzes
Test your knowledge

Share
Share titles within your Learning Management System (LMS) or Library Circulation System

Citation
Create bibliographical references following the Chicago Manual of Style

ATLANTA FALCONS CONTENTS

Matt Ryan has played for the Falcons his entire NFL career.

INTRODUCTION

The Atlanta Falcons joined the National Football League (NFL) in 1965. Since then, the team has reached the **Super Bowl** twice. Behind quarterback Matt Ryan, the Falcons have become one of the best teams in the National Football Conference (NFC). Their high-powered offense has kept fans entertained for years.

ATLANTA FALCONS

Stadium Mercedes-Benz Stadium

Division National Football Conference (NFC) South

Head Coach Arthur Smith

Location Atlanta, Georgia

Super Bowl Titles 0

Nicknames Dirty Birds, Grits Blitz

14 Playoff Appearances

2 Super Bowl Appearances

6 Division Championships

OVERTIME

The Falcons outscored the Patriots in the first half of Super Bowl LI, but the Patriots tied the game in the second half. It was the first ever Super Bowl to go into overtime.

HISTORY

The Atlanta Falcons started playing in 1966. They struggled in their first season. The Falcons only won three games. However, they improved over time. In 1978, the team went 9–7 and played in their first **postseason**.

In 1998, quarterback Chris Chandler led the team to their first Super Bowl appearance. Unfortunately, they lost to the Denver Broncos. In the 2016 season, the team reached the Super Bowl again. They held a lead for much of the game before losing to the New England Patriots.

Chris Chandler led the Falcons to a 14–2 record in 1998.

The popular fan cheer "Rise Up!" comes from the lyrics of a gospel song.

THE STADIUM

Mercedes-Benz Stadium opened in 2017. It has the largest video board in the world. It also has a **retractable roof**. This allows the Falcons to play in any weather conditions.

The stadium is used for many events. College football games are played there. Mercedes-Benz Stadium is also used for soccer games. In 2019, the stadium hosted the Super Bowl. The New England Patriots beat the Los Angeles Rams.

More than 70,000 people filled Mercedes-Benz Stadium in 2019 to watch the Super Bowl.

Falcons fans can enjoy the stadium's signature Chicken in a Waffle Bowl with a side of waffle fries between quarters at Mercedes-Benz Stadium.

WHERE THEY PLAY

Mercedes-Benz STADIUM

NATIONAL FOOTBALL CONFERENCE

East

1 **Dallas Cowboys** AT&T Stadium
2 **New York Giants** MetLife Stadium
3 **Philadelphia Eagles** Lincoln Financial Field
4 **Washington Football Team** FedEx Field

North

5 **Chicago Bears** Soldier Field
6 **Detroit Lions** Ford Field
7 **Green Bay Packers** Lambeau Field
8 **Minnesota Vikings** U.S. Bank Stadium

South

9 **Atlanta Falcons** Mercedes-Benz Stadium
10 **Carolina Panthers** Bank of America Stadium
11 **New Orleans Saints** Mercedes-Benz Superdome
12 **Tampa Bay Buccaneers** Raymond James Stadium

West

13 **Arizona Cardinals** State Farm Stadium
14 **Los Angeles Rams** SoFi Stadium
15 **San Francisco 49ers** Levi's Stadium
16 **Seattle Seahawks** Lumen Field

RING OF HONOR

The Falcons do not retire jersey numbers. The team's Ring of Honor recognizes individual players by name instead of number. There have been 11 Falcons named to the Ring of Honor.

THE UNIFORMS

The Atlanta Falcons' first uniforms had either black or white jerseys. Players wore white pants. There was a falcon **logo** on the sleeves of the jerseys. In 2004, red became the main jersey color. The black jerseys became the **alternate jerseys**. These "throwback" jerseys were worn for a few special games each season.

In 2020, the uniforms changed. Black became the color for home games once again. The away uniforms were changed to white with white pants. There is also a red and black alternate jersey.

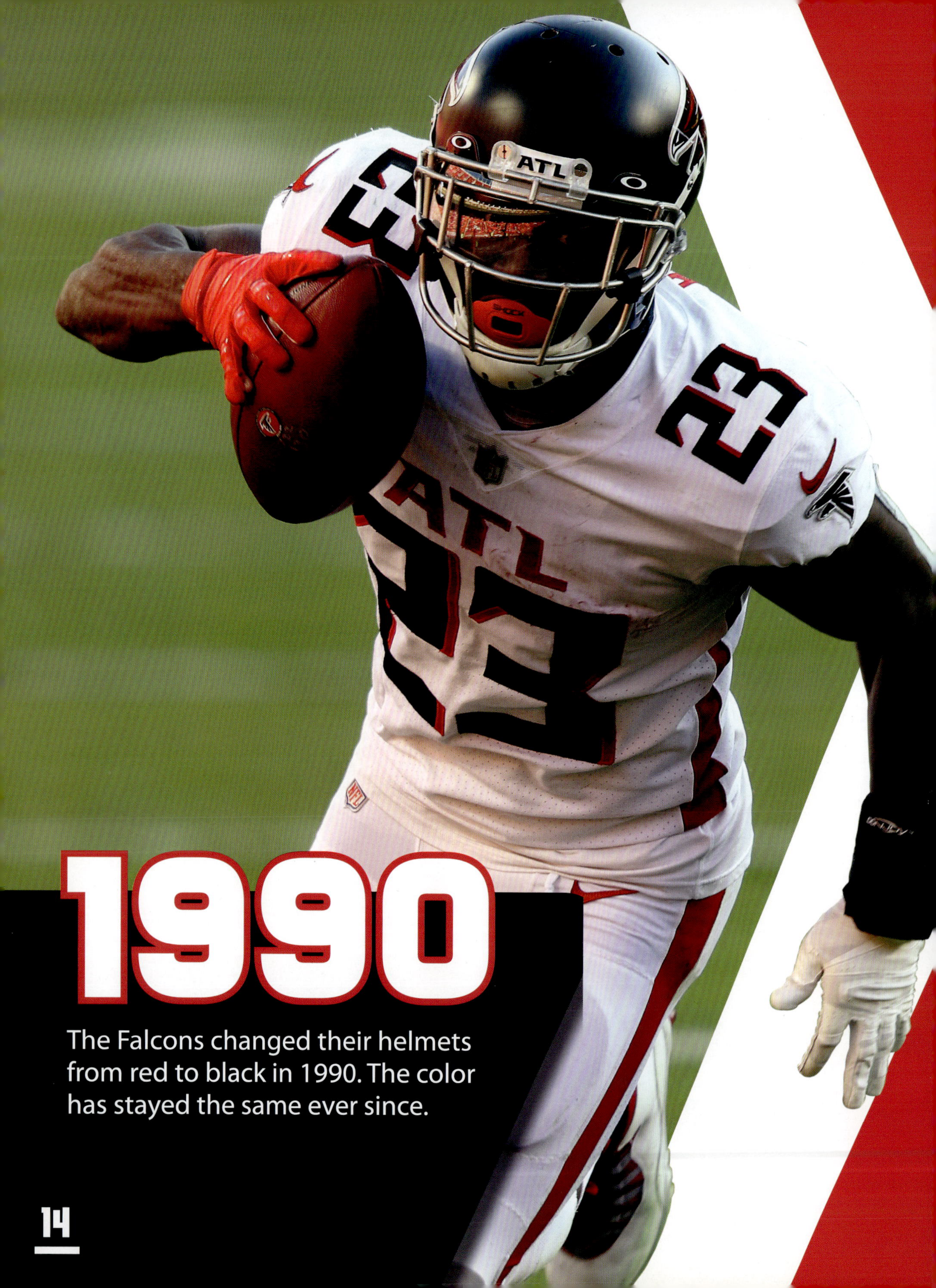

1990

The Falcons changed their helmets from red to black in 1990. The color has stayed the same ever since.

THE HELMETS

At first, the Falcons wore red helmets with a black falcon logo. There was a black stripe in the center of the helmet. It was surrounded by two gold stripes and two white stripes.

In 2003, the logo was changed to include red and silver accents. This new design was meant to look like a fierce bird of prey. In addition, the new logo looked more like the capital letter "F" for "Falcons." Since this redesign, the fiercer Falcons logo has remained unchanged. In 2020, the logo was enlarged, and the black was changed from glossy to matte.

Many football helmets now include sensors. They record the force and direction of impact of the hits a player receives during a game.

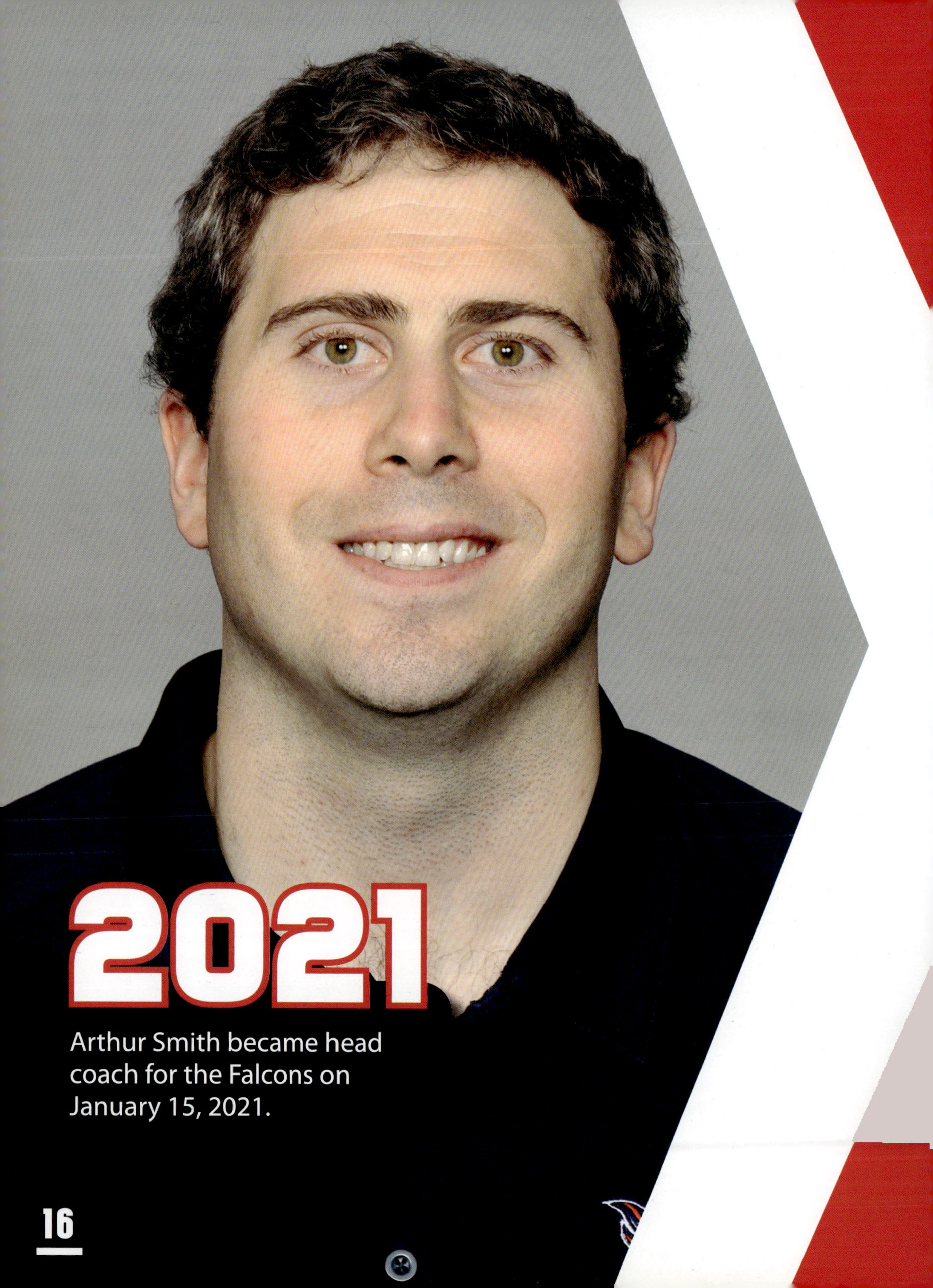

2021

Arthur Smith became head coach for the Falcons on January 15, 2021.

THE COACHES

The Falcons have a long tradition of skillful head coaches. The team has had twelve full-time coaches since 1966. From Jerry Glanville to Arthur Smith, the Falcons' coaching staff have worked very hard to bring out their players' best qualities.

Jerry Glanville Jerry Glanville designed a **Run-N-Shoot** offense and favored aggressive play on defense. Under Glanville, the 1991 Falcons won 10 regular-season games. They also had their first playoff victory in nearly 15 years.

Dan Reeves Dan Reeves was a player before he coached. He made a total of nine trips to the Super Bowl with the Dallas Cowboys. In Atlanta, he coached the team to Super Bowl XXXIII.

Dan Quinn Dan Quinn left the Seattle Seahawks in 2015 to lead the Falcons. In just his second season, he led the team to the Super Bowl. Quinn coached the Falcons until 2020.

Freddie Falcon makes surprise visits to tailgaters and other fans on game days.

THE MASCOT

Freddie Falcon is popular on social media, with thousands of followers on Instagram.

Freddie Falcon was the first professional mascot in the history of Atlanta. He has been a familiar face around the city for more than 35 years. He even delivers "Freddie-Grams" around the city on Valentine's Day. They include a dozen roses, a box of chocolates, a Freddie Falcon doll, and an Atlanta Falcons T-shirt.

While Freddie is a devoted football fan, he also appears at elementary schools across the state. He encourages students to make healthy decisions, play outside for 60 minutes daily, and study hard.

Falcons fans know it is time to start cheering when they see Freddie waving the team's flag on the field.

LEGENDS OF THE PAST

Many great players have suited up in the Falcons' red and black. A few of them have become icons of the team and the city it represents.

Michael Turner

Falcons fans had no idea just how quickly Michael Turner's presence would pay off in 2008. In his first game as a Falcon, he rushed for a team-record 220 yards and 2 touchdowns. Turner's 17 rushing touchdowns in the 2008 season set a new single-season record for the team.

Born February 13, 1982, in Waukegan, Illinois
Position Running Back
9 NFL Seasons (2004–2012)

Jamal Anderson

Jamal Anderson's breakout season came in 1998, when he rushed for 14 touchdowns and a Falcons' record 1,846 yards. He made the "Dirty Bird" touchdown dance popular. This celebration involved flapping his arms as though they were wings. Fans mimicked this all across the country.

Born September 30, 1972, in Newark, New Jersey
Position Running Back
8 NFL Seasons (1994–2001)

Deion Sanders

Deion Sanders is also known as "Prime Time" Deion and "Neon." He is considered by many to be the best cornerback ever to play in the NFL. He was known for his speed, his ability to shut down the game's best receivers, and his ability to find the end zone.

Born August 9, 1967, in Fort Myers, Florida
Position Cornerback
14 NFL Seasons
(1989–2000; 2004–2005)

MODERN STARS

In recent years, the Falcons' team has included many young, talented players. They have proven that they are among the best in the league.

Grady Jarrett

Grady Jarrett has spent his entire NFL career with the Falcons. During his rookie season, he totaled 24 tackles. During the 2020 season, Jarrett made 27 solo tackles and 4 **sacks**. He was invited to the Pro Bowl for the first time in 2019, and again in 2020.

Born April 28, 1993, in Conyers, Georgia
Position Defensive Tackle
NFL Seasons 2015–present

Matt Ryan

Matt Ryan's nickname is "Matty Ice" because of his ability to remain calm under pressure. He has been setting records in Atlanta since his first season. Ryan led the NFL in completion percentage in 2012, with 68.6 percent. He has set new Falcons single-season records, including 439 pass completions, 4,944 passing yards, and 38 passing touchdowns.

Born May 17, 1985, in Exton, Pennsylvania
Position Quarterback
NFL Seasons 2008–present

Julio Jones

Coming off a spectacular season for **Bowl Championship Series (BCS)** National Champion Alabama Crimson Tide, hopes were high for Julio Jones. Jones exceeded them all. He caught 20 touchdown passes in his first 34 games with the Falcons. In 2013, his third year in the league, he averaged 116 receiving yards per game.

Born February 8, 1989, in Foley, Alabama
Position Wide Receiver
NFL Seasons 2011–present

ALL-TIME RECORDS

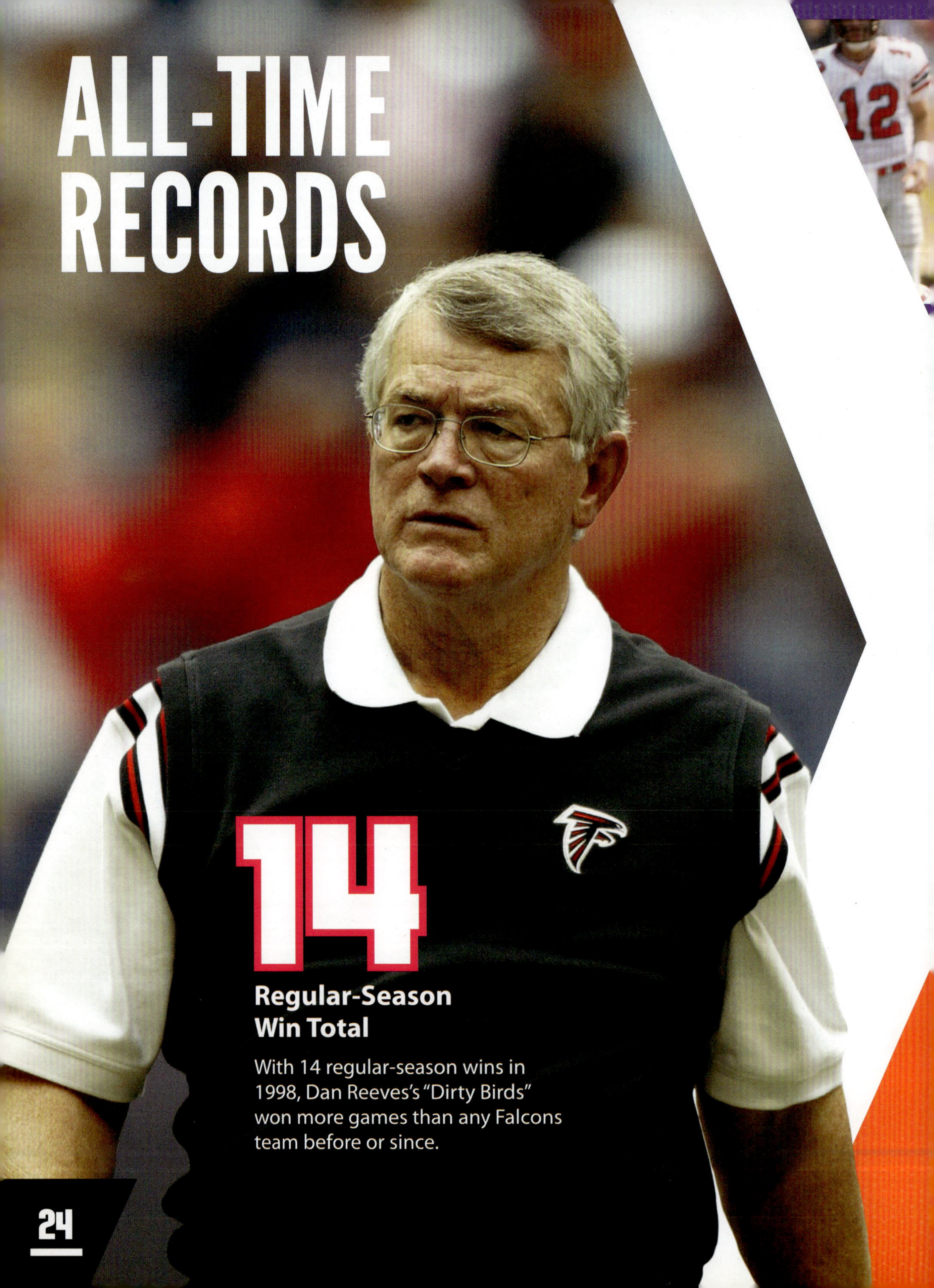

14

Regular-Season Win Total

With 14 regular-season wins in 1998, Dan Reeves's "Dirty Birds" won more games than any Falcons team before or since.

6,631

All-Time Rushing Yards

Gerald Riggs's three straight 1,000-yard rushing seasons in the mid-1980s helped him become the team's all-time rushing leader.

39

Career Interceptions

Cornerback Rolland Lawrence snagged 39 interceptions, a Falcons record, during his time with the team in the 1970s.

60

All-Time Rushing Touchdowns

Michael Turner holds the Falcons' record for the most rushing touchdowns. He also set the single-season touchdown record in 2008, with 17.

16.5

Single-Season Sacks

With 16.5 sacks in 2008, Falcons linebacker John Abraham set the team's all-time single-season mark.

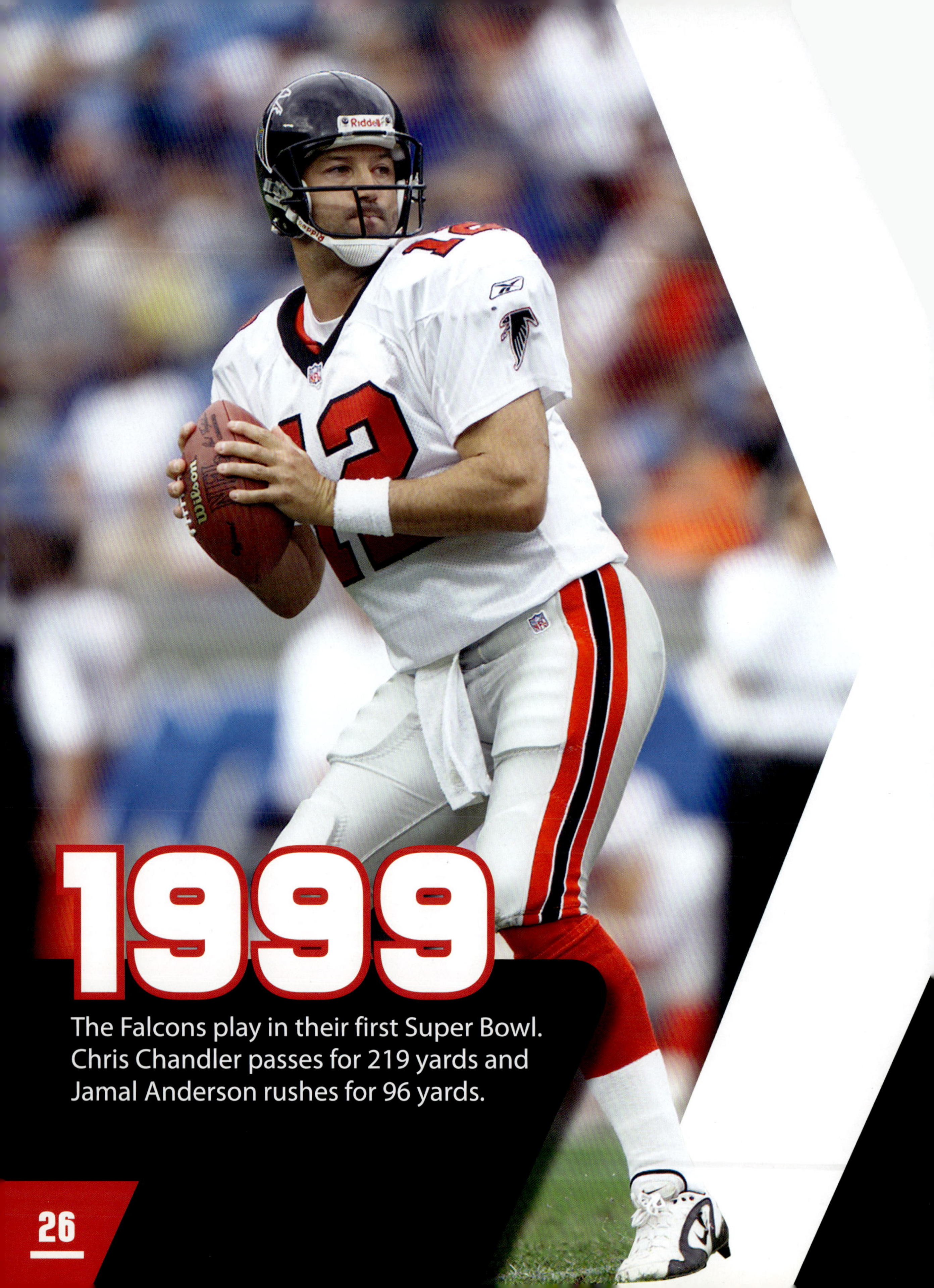

1999

The Falcons play in their first Super Bowl. Chris Chandler passes for 219 yards and Jamal Anderson rushes for 96 yards.

FALCONS TIMELINE

Throughout the team's history, the Atlanta Falcons have had many memorable events. These have become defining moments for the team and its fans.

1965 The Falcons are founded. NFL Commissioner Pete Rozelle grants ownership to Rankin M. Smith Sr.

1971 Norm Van Brocklin coaches the Falcons to a 7–6–1 win-loss-tie record. It is the first winning record in the team's history.

1991 The Falcons win 10 games and make the playoffs for the first time in nine years.

2017 The Falcons reach the Super Bowl. However, they lose to the New England Patriots.

2019 The team drafts guard Chris Lindstrom 14th overall to shore up their offensive line for the future.

WRITE A BIOGRAPHY

Life Story
A person's life story can be the subject of a book. This kind of book is called a biography. Reading a biography can help you learn more about a great person.

Get the Facts
Use this book, and research in the library and on the internet, to find out more about your favorite Falcon.

Read the questions in the concept web on the following page. Answer the questions in your notebook. Your answers will help you write a biography.

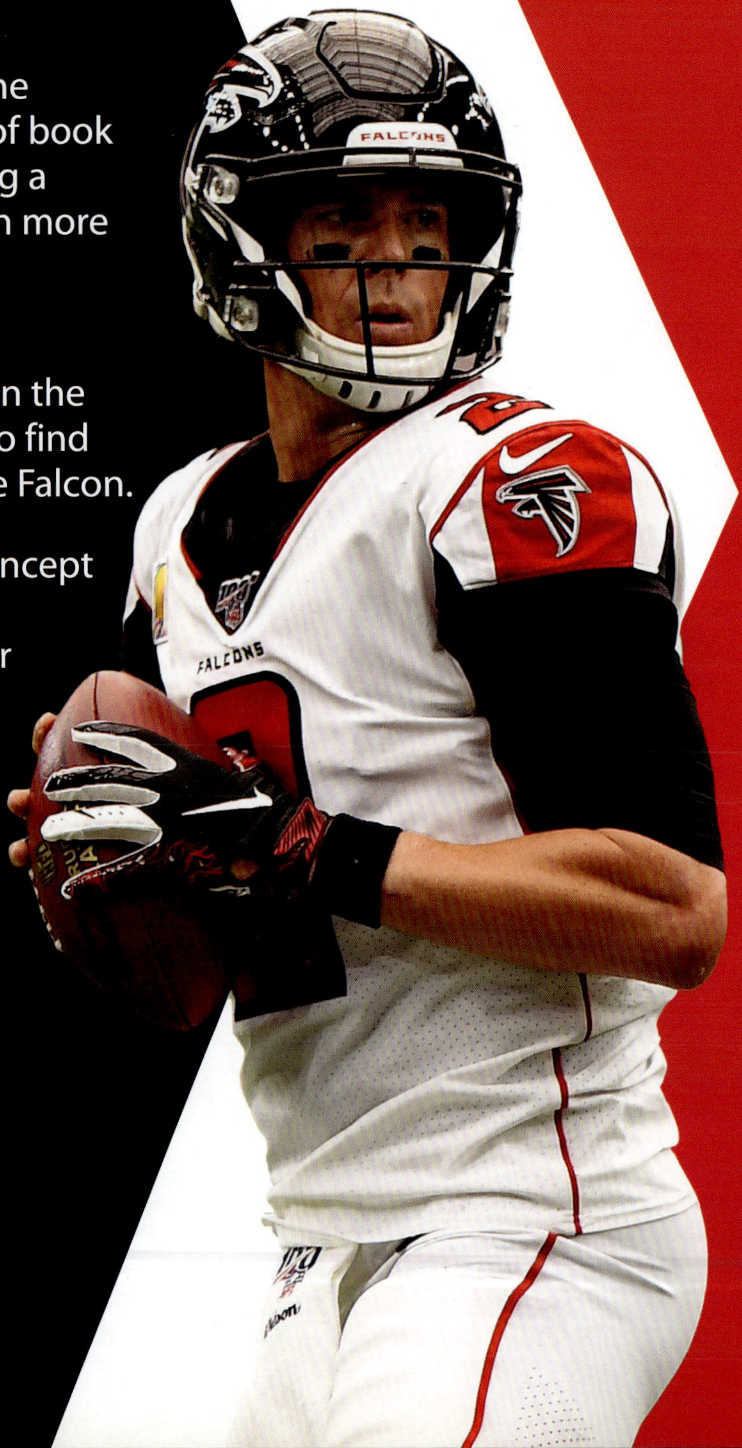

CONCEPT WEB

WRITE A BIOGRAPHY

Adulthood
- Where does this person live?
- Does he have a family?

Your Opinion
- What did you learn from the books you read in your research?
- Was anything missing from these books?

Childhood
- Where and when was this person born?
- Describe his parents, siblings, and friends.

Accomplishments off the Field
- What is this person's life's work?
- How have this person's accomplishments served others?

Help and Obstacles
- What obstacles did this person face?
- Did he receive help from others?
- Did this person have a positive attitude?

Accomplishments on the Field
- What records does this person hold?
- What are his key games and plays?
- What are his most important stats?

Work and Preparation
- What was this person's education?
- What was his work experience?

TRIVIA TIME

1 In what year did the Falcons have their first winning record?

2 How many wins did the Falcons have in 1998?

3 Which former Atlanta player is considered by many to be the best cornerback ever to play in the NFL?

4 In what year did the Falcons start playing in the NFL?

5 Who holds the Falcons' record for single-season sacks?

6 Who was the coach of the Falcons in their last Super Bowl?

7 What color are the Falcons' 2020 home uniforms?

8 Who has the most rushing touchdowns in Falcons history?

ANSWERS

1. 1971
2. 14
3. Deion Sanders
4. 1966
5. John Abraham
6. Dan Quinn
7. Black
8. Michael Turner

KEY WORDS

alternate jerseys: jerseys that sports teams may wear in games instead of their home or away uniforms

Bowl Championship Series (BCS): an arrangement of five American college postseason football games that determines the national champion

logo: a symbol that stands for a team or organization

postseason: the period following the end of the regular season

retractable roof: a roof that can move from an open position into a closed position that completely covers the field of play and spectator areas

Run-N-Shoot: a freewheeling style of offense in football that emphasizes passing

sacks: when quarterbacks are tackled behind the line of scrimmage before they can throw a forward pass

Super Bowl: the NFL's annual championship game between the winning team from the NFC and the winning team from the AFC

INDEX

Published by AV2
276 5th Avenue
Suite 704 #917
New York, NY 10001
Website: www.av2books.com

Library of Congress Control Number: 2020931703

ISBN 978-1-7911-2439-7 (hardcover)
ISBN 978-1-7911-2440-3 (multi-user eBook)

Printed in Guangzhou, China
1 2 3 4 5 6 7 8 9 0 25 24 23 22 21

052021
101320

Art Director: Terry Paulhus Project Coordinator: John Willis

Every reasonable effort has been made to trace ownership and to obtain permission to reprint copyright material. The publisher would be pleased to have any errors or omissions brought to its attention so that they may be corrected in subsequent printings.

The publisher acknowledges Alamy, Getty Images, Newscom, and Wikimedia as the primary image suppliers for this title.